Power Down & Parent Up!
Cyber Bullying, Screen Dependence & Raising Tech-Healthy Children

By Holli Kenley, M.A., Marriage & Family Therapist

Foreword by Laurie Zelinger, PhD and Fred Zelinger, PhD

Loving Healing Press

Ann Arbor

Power Down & Parent Up!: Cyber Bullying, Screen Dependence &
Raising Tech-Healthy Children
Copyright © 2017, 2019 by Holli Kenley. All Rights Reserved.
Foreword by Laurie Zelinger, PhD and Fred Zelinger, PhD

Library of Congress Cataloging-in-Publication Data

Names: Kenley, Holli, 1951- author.
Title: Power down & parent up! : cyber bullying, screen dependence & raising
  tech-healthy children / by Holli Kenley, M.A., Marriage & Family Therapist
  ; foreword by Laurie Zelinger, PhD and Fred Zelinger, PhD.
Other titles: Power down and parent up!
Description: 1st Edition. | Ann Arbor, MI : Loving Healing Press, [2017] |
  "Part One of this book was originally published as standalone monograph
  "Cyber Bullying No More: Parenting a High Tech Generation" (2011)" |
  Includes bibliographical references and index.
Identifiers: LCCN 2017023889 (print) | LCCN 2017036554 (ebook) | ISBN
  9781615993512 (ePub, PDF, Kindle) | ISBN 9781615993505 (pbk. : alk. paper)
Subjects: LCSH: Cyberbullying. | Internet and children--Safety measures. |
  Internet and children--Safety measures. | Internet--Psychological aspects.
Classification: LCC HV6773.15.C92 (ebook) | LCC HV6773.15.C92 K46 2017
  (print) | DDC 302.34/302854678--dc23
LC record available at https://lccn.loc.gov/2017023889

Now available in audiobook formats from Audible and iTunes!

Distributed by Ingram Book Group (USA/CAN/AU), Bertram's Book
(UK/EU)

Published by
Loving Healing Press
5145 Pontiac Trail
Ann Arbor, MI 48105

Tollfree 888-761-6268
Fax 734-663-6861

www.LHPress.com
info@LHPress.com

Contents

Why Should We Care?

We are fortunate to live at a time of technological advancement and wonder. Each day brings new discoveries and devices, enabling us to communicate and socialize with ease. However, as we embrace new technologies and their inherent benefits, we also must remain open to their possible consequences. For example, cyber bullying is not a cause of maladaptive social behavior. It is a behavioral consequence resulting from a complex, dynamic relationship between individuals and their electronic devices. In the past five years, our digital world has grown exponentially as has the degree of time both adults and children spend on their screens. Not surprisingly, researchers are discovering a myriad of unhealthy manifestations associated with excessive screen time, especially for children.

We have three goals in *Power Down & Parent Up*. First, parents/guardians, we will "Power Down," turning our full attention to cyber bullying. We will begin taking control of our children's health by implementing a concise "Parent Up" approach in tackling cyber bullying, applying proven strategies for Protection, Intervention, and Prevention. Second, we will "Power Down" and tackle screen dependence, becoming focused and fully informed about growing health concerns and consequences. Third, by embracing a program of *Seven Proactive Practices* and *Four Healthy Guidelines,* we will "Parent Up" as we continue to take control of our children's health.

Part One: Let's Tackle Cyber Bullying

Foreword

Bullying is an issue occurring with increasing frequency and consequence within the lives of our children, a phenomenon witnessed regularly in our role as school psychologists, private practice therapists, and as parents. Significant levels of attention are now being given within schools in an effort to stem the tide, empower victims, and deflate the aggressors. Many schools have made a commitment to eradicating this pattern of reprehensible behavior, and have adopted formal programs to raise awareness by actively involving students and parents in reducing, reporting and preventing bullying. Schools deal with the face-to-face issues taking place during school hours, and at times, even those incidents reported outside of school when the effects spill over into the school day.

However, issues arising through venues beyond school hours are often left to families to handle. How many parents are actually prepared to recognize and address bullying when it occurs through the Internet, texting or social media avenues? Youngsters often conceal such things from "prying" parental eyes. It is especially concerning because, as Kenley cites in this book, "Many experts suggest that children do not report being violated online for fear of having their technology taken away or fear of retaliation" Likewise, she teaches us that children's technological level of savvy for their age far surpasses their ability to make sound judgments regarding potential risks of on-line communication.

The exploding social network brought to us by the rapidly advancing technology supporting the Internet has altered the very fabric of human communication and interaction. Geographical distances are no longer a roadblock to immediate contact, and millions of people can be accessed simultaneously and instantly. Face-to-face discussions are being replaced by pixels on a screen and visually deciphered symbols and words in the absence of facial expression, physical demeanor, or vocal inflexion. The sender can decide to be anonymous, or if clever, easily disguised as someone else. Like most change, the revolution in communication brought to us by millions of linked computers and phones carries with it both amazing benefits, and frightening pitfalls. This book provides us with a powerful, accurate, and concise description of the already prevalent concern known as "cyber bullying," also providing us with a well-thought-out conceptualization of what parents can do.

In this "no holds barred" manual, Kenley has captured the incredible significance and power of cyber bullying, in a way that leaves the reader both shaken by its impact, and relieved by the steps offered to manage it. This booklet is not an expression of fear or worry; rather it is a brilliant effort to provide parents with the tools and concepts they need to both understand the potentials of internet communication, and those needed to protect and assist their children in using technology effectively and safely. She makes her point quickly, thoroughly and accurately, leaving the reader feeling able to better understand, communicate and protect children in a world with so many unknowns.

Laurie Zelinger, PhD, RPT-S and Fred Zelinger, PhD:
Licensed Psychologists

Cyber Bullying: An Alarming Reality

There has been much in the news over the past several years about the dangers and abuses of online behaviors. Many harmful actions come from the classmates, friends, and peers of our children rather than from strangers or predators. Bullying, which has caused significant injury in the lives of countless victims throughout the years, has now become a relentless and horrifically destructive cyber force. As kids embrace a world magically transformed by the wonders of technology, they also enter into an electronic culture void of human regard for one another; and tragically, they often find themselves navigating through a climate infused with revenge, retaliation and regret.

With one out of every five children having been the target of cyber bullying (Patchin & Hinduja, 2011), educators, psychologists, civil leaders and legal experts have been working tirelessly developing programs to combat it. In addition, professionals in a myriad of fields are developing strategies to intervene on behalf of the victims while searching for ways to hold the perpetrators accountable. However, every day, countless numbers of individuals fall prey to the abusive behaviors generated through social networking sites and other electronic means of communication. Sadly, as is often the case, parents/guardians who are struggling with the stressors and responsibilities of everyday life know little about the online bullying culture, or are aware of the importance of their role in parenting a high-tech generation.

Although there are dozens of books, videos, websites, and resources available for help in dealing with cyber bullying, the purposes of this article are to give parents/guardians a manageable number of principles and practices to incorporate into their daily lives. The parenting strategies will cover three areas of importance: Protection, Intervention, and Prevention.

Protection

Today's young people are growing up on a diet of technology with immediate access to worldwide social connections. Because it has become so common in our society for them to have a cell phone, laptop, iPhone, or iPad, etc., we sometimes forget about the window of danger this opens. Parents would never hand over the car keys to their teens without the required number of education courses, behind-the-wheel practice hours, and supervision by an adult. And yet, we put a cell phone or a laptop in the hands of young children without adequate preparation, instruction or monitoring. We can begin protecting our high-tech children by implementing several safety measures into our parenting.

1. Know why you are giving your children access to a piece of technology or giving them permission to utilize the technology

One excellent tool of measurement as to when a child should be given a piece of technology is for the parent/guardian to have a valid reason for doing so. These reasons might include providing for the safety of children or for emergency contacts. Caving into peer pressure or your child's rebellious attitude is never an example of responsible parenting. As children age, more access to different kinds of technology is appropriate. Again, check your adult rationale for doing so. However, with each device, parents must gradually guide their children through the various electronic mediums and venues. If your child made a new friend you'd want to know where he is going, what he is doing. The same is true with this piece of technology. Teach your children how to navigate through the new territory. If you are like many parents/guardians who are not as tech savvy as their children, have them share their web world with you while discussing and implementing safety measures.

2. Clearly explain the rules and expectations about the use of technology

Families need to take time to talk about how to use technology responsibly. Handing it over without instruction is leading your child blindly into a dangerous environment. Whatever the device, develop a set of rules and expectations about its usage:

- What is it to be used for?
- How often can it be used?
- When and where is it not to be used?

- What costs are being incurred? Who will pay?
- Who or what may be contacted? Who or what is not to be contacted?

It is mandatory that parents/guardians establish an "internet use agreement" with their children. Examples can be found and downloaded from:

- *Family Online Internet Safety Contract*
  www.fosi.org/resources.html

- *Family Internet Use Contract and Cell Phone Use Contract*
  www.cyberbullying.us/cyberbullying_internet_use_contract.pdf

- *Family Contract for Online Safety*
  www.safekids.com/family-contact-for-online-safety (Patchin & Hinduja, 2011).

Although it seems like a lot of energy and time to hammer out an agreement or to put one into place, remember that we are talking about the safety of children. Like most issues in parenting, doing the hard work upfront often saves everyone from tremendous heartache in the end.

3. Monitor the use of the technology

When parents/guardians have established some ground rules for use of technology, they have a foundation from which to monitor the agreed-upon expectations. This serves as an excellent communication tool to revise and revisit needs as they change or evolve. Parents often think that less supervision is needed as children get older. However, research shows that the more young people become proficient on the computer, the more likely they are to engage in cyber bullying, or to be victimized. We also know that children's knowledge of technology in relationship to their respective ages far surpasses their ability to make evaluative or analytical judgments regarding the dangers and risks of online behaviors. Keeping this in mind, parents/guardians do not need to be constantly monitoring their children, but it is vital to check frequently and do so with careful examination. Other helpful hints include:

- Keeping computers, laptops, etc. within the family room, kitchen, etc. Have them visible!
- No "after hours" usage (refer to family contract).
- Talk openly about the kinds of activities, sites, etc. your children are using, discovering, avoiding, etc.

4. Implement safety measures

In the early stages of introducing your children to healthy online communication, implement the following safety measures:

- Protect passwords. Teach children not to share their passwords.
- Protect profiles. Teach children to limit the amount and kinds of information posted online. Also, utilize the security setting provided by online social sites.
- Obtain filtering and monitoring software.
- Monitor your child's online reputation.

5. Establish a net neighborhood

In her book *The Bully, The Bullied, and The Bystander* (2008), Barbara Coloroso strongly suggests that parents/guardians embrace technology in the same manner as they would when introducing their children to a new neighborhood. Some of her suggestions include:

- Parents/guardians need to get to know the net neighborhood. Educate yourselves and know who and what you are dealing with. Once again, if you find yourself struggling with the cyber world, have your children teach you!
- As young children begin to venture out, supervise them and explore with them!
- As children grow and mature, give them more freedom, but explain the risks as well as the responsibilities that come with that independence.
- Get to know your children's web buddies, just as you would their friends.
- Understand that your children have a "relationship" with the web. Your oversight is no less important than if it were your child's first serious boyfriend/girlfriend.
- Keep communication channels open; let your children know you are there for them, no matter what.

6. Negotiate and renegotiate the rules as age, responsibility, and needs change

Although there are numerous theories and views on effective parenting strategies, many psychologists and clinicians agree that *authoritative* parenting commonly produces the healthiest outcomes. Authoritative parenting involves a flexible blend of following rules, of accepting responsibilities for one's behavior, and of compassionate, respectful dialogue between parents and children. Structure and direction are woven into a nurturing approach. As issues surface around technology, children and parents need to deal with them openly and with meaningful accountability. Keep in mind these additional parenting strategies:

- Avoid punishing your children for the online behaviors of others.
- Avoid establishing rules and consequences that cannot be implemented.
- Avoid over-reacting to online misbehaviors. Keep the severity of the issue in mind as you administer a consequence. Remember, it is important for children to have the opportunity to correct their behaviors and to learn from their mistakes rather than to develop a rebellious spirit toward authority.

7. Parents — model healthy behaviors with technology, and obey the laws in place

Parents, we are our children's best teachers of what to do or what not to do. We must model healthy and appropriate behaviors with technology. And we must obey the laws within our respective cities, states, and countries.

Intervention

Even with safeguards in place and teaching your children to use technology in responsible, meaningful ways, there are no guarantees that they will not become victims or perpetrators of cyber bullying. Even with anti-bullying laws in 45 states, including 31 states specifying *electronic harassment,* only 6 states specifically include laws against *cyber bullying* (Patchin & Hinduja, 2011). In addition, although there are 43 states that *require school policies* (Patchin & Hinduja, 2011) addressing bullying and cyber bullying, many schools find themselves unable to implement such policies due to lack of resources, funding, or manpower to follow up on the many violations. Therefore, instead of expending a great deal of energy blaming others for their lack of responsibility in addressing a cyber bullying attack, or relying solely on external sources to remedy the injury, parents need to be on the frontline of intervention.

1. Have a safety plan in place

Families must have a safety plan in place and it should be discussed with all family members. One of the most effective plans in response to being cyber bullied is the following (Hanel & Trolley, 2010):

- **Stop** what you are doing. Don't respond or react to the bullying behavior.
- **Save** the information. Do not delete. Print out a hard copy.
- **Share** the information with an adult you can trust and who can help you make a safe decision on how to handle the situation.

Many experts suggest that children fail to report being violated online for fear of having their technology taken away or fear of retaliation. In lieu of having their technology removed or grounding children from it, parents/guardians may do the following:

- Block senders of abusive or inappropriate messages, photos, etc.
- Request that the website or social networking site remove the offensive material.
- If necessary, contact school personnel or legal authorities.
- Change passwords when violated.
- Take down profiles or remove self from online site or venue.

2. Let your children know that it is safe and necessary that they come to you (or another trusted adult) if they are cyber bullied

It is extremely important that children do not feel alone when victimized. Research has suggested that they are reluctant to disclose being cyber bullied because nothing is done to help them even after it has been reported to an adult. Take time to talk with them about how they are feeling; help them to implement the appropriate safety measures (discussed in #2); and continue to monitor their online reputations. Above all, be available and be supportive.

3. Understand the difference between web buddies and real friends

Children today have countless numbers of online acquaintances. It often becomes difficult for them to differentiate between web buddies and real friends. With peers changing their friendship status as easily as changing a pair of shoes and with online bullying being so prevalent, it is quite confusing for children to understand what a *real friend is*. As parents, it is our duty to teach them about the characteristics of true friendship, and of the importance of how we treat one another. Helping them to understand that real friends do not betray one another (through bullying or other means) will help children in clarifying their confusion and in moving through their hurt.

Tragically, research has also suggested that many children who do not see a difference between the real world and the cyber world find it completely natural to treat others inhumanely (Li, 2010). The thinking is that if the damaging behavior online can be acted out with limited consequences, it is permissible to do so in person. Thus, it is all the more important for us to spend time with our children, talking about the harmful effects of online and offline bullying and of the real person at the receiving end of such attacks.

4. Take advantage of counseling or support groups

In the past several years, many young people have taken their own lives because of relentless, abusive acts of cyber bullying. It is extremely important for a child who is experiencing ongoing victimization to seek out support from a school counselor, professional therapist, or an age-appropriate support group. Victims tend to withdraw, become depressed, and feel completely lost and isolated. Do not hide behind the belief that the bullying will go away or will just get better over time. It will not.

In addition to person-to-person support, there are a couple of excellent websites available to help and support young people who have questions about bullying or who are being targeted (Patchin & Hinduja, 2011). These sites are interactive, where children can connect with others who have experienced similar experiences:

- *Cyberbullying 411:* www.cyberbyllying.com
- *Cyber Mentors:* http://cybermentors.org.uk

5. Be aware of retaliation and of the relationship between victims and bullies

In their research, Kowalski, Limber, and Agatston (2008) have shown that there is a strong relationship between traditional bullies, cyber bullies, cyber bully victims, and victims. For example, if a child is exhibiting traditional bullying behaviors, it is likely that he is also bullying others online, and he may even be a victim of cyber bullying. We also know that cyber victims frequently cross over to cyber bullying behaviors. And yet, there are times when individuals are "pure victims" or "pure bullies," with no other roles being played out. This is important information for us as we investigate the child's involvement in bullying behaviors, and seek out effective interventions.

Regardless of a child's relationship with cyber bullying, it is never a healthy option to seek revenge or to continue the retaliation. Teaching kids how to protect and take care of themselves as well as how to treat others respectfully serves them, and is a critical step toward curtailing rampant cyber bullying.

6. Continue to talk with your children, monitor activities, and negotiate or amend rules as needed

Stay involved with your children and in their relationship with technology. Don't assume that everything is alright — *know that it is.* Revisit your "family contract or agreement" from time to time. Make changes or additions as circumstances, age, and needs dictate. Use the topic of technology as a vehicle to stay connected to your children, to communicate with them, and to demonstrate how much you care about their worlds — real and cyber.

Prevention

Even after someone has completed driver's training, passed driving exams, and has shown the maturity and responsibility to drive a car, these preparatory safety measures will not prevent an accident. This is a painful realization, but true. Although it is not always possible or even realistic, as carers for kids, we must acknowledge that the only way to absolutely prevent our children from being injured by someone or something is to never allow them access to that person or thing. It is absurd to entertain the idea of excluding technology from our society, but we can have an honest discussion about the destructive behaviors nurtured by electronic communication, and we can learn how those behaviors are reinforced by the workings of technology. By educating ourselves about the *causal factors* of a cyber bullying culture, we can open our minds to healthier ways of interacting and relearning social ways of being. So, we can begin to eradicate the breeding grounds of this contagious pathogen and prevent its spread.

1. Educate yourself and your children about the relationship between technology and the individual, and its impact on us as social beings

This is extremely important. When children communicate through any electronic source, they participate in an *indirect relationship*. In other words, they are not *face to face* with someone else. This dynamic of being separated from the presence of another human being creates feelings of detachment. As these feelings of detachment and disconnect take hold, two additional forces come into play: anonymity and power differential. Given these two forces, a child is at liberty to say whatever he wants, to as many people as he likes, with no feedback as to how damaging or injurious the words may be to the victim. Over time and with repeated usage of electronic means of communication, our children's psychological makeup is indeed impacted. Studies in Singapore suggest that "technology reduces the sensitivity an individual has toward others and his/her environment." (Ang & Goh, 2010). Other important developmental changes include the following:

- Children experience a disconnect from the *real* world and with *real* relationships (Hinduja & Patchin, 2009).
- Children's behaviors become increasingly disinhibited (Dooley, Pyzalski, & Cross, 2009). Due to a lack of oversight, children feel more freedom to express themselves in inappropriate ways.
- Children experience a loss of empathy for others or lack of human regard for one another (Ang & Goh, 2010).
- Children begin to exhibit feelings of contempt: a sense of entitlement, intolerance toward differences, and a liberty to exclude others (Colorosso, 2008).
- Children demonstrate a decline in positive social/personal interaction or in the development of healthy social skills (Ang & Goh, 2010).

Although these characteristics may seem unimportant or insignificant in the overall development of a child, with continued online usage without the balance of interpersonal communication, these ways of thinking show themselves as antisocial and narcissistic personas called *cyber bullies*. And, as these unhealthy personalities permeate the cyber world, they fuel and feed the online bullying culture.

2. Educate yourself and your children about how technology itself reinforces unhealthy behaviors

As children experience feelings of autonomy, of power, and of detachment in their cyber world, and as they develop unhealthy behaviors and characteristics, they an their parents are largely unaware of how the technology itself conditions and reinforces those behaviors. In other words, technology sustains and motivates the bullying persona in the following ways (Hinduja & Patchin, 2009):

- There is no immediate feedback loop or consequence to deter the bully from the behavior. Moreover, there is little or no accountability for wrongdoing.
- The bully does not have face-to-face contact with the victim. Therefore, he is removed from the impact on the victim, which typically acts as a deterrent to aggressive behaviors.
- The bullying act gains infamy by remaining online for lengthy periods of time with countless users weighing in. This serves to empower the bully.

- The bully is protected through anonymity, pseudonymity, and fake profiles. Again, there is no consequence or accountability for the behavior.

- Because of the ease of responding, technology erases the "reflection time" typically used to think through or to evaluate an action. This is replaced with habitual impulsivity.

- Although more research is needed, there is a suggestion that the bully's behavior is reinforced by the "sense of anticipation/ excitement he experiences between the sending of the attack and the time when the victim actually is made aware of the attack." (Dooley, Pyzalski, & Cross, 2009, p .186).

- Although the role of bystanders varies, many bullies are motivated/ empowered by offline and online participants (Li, 2010).

We adults must acknowledge that although there are countless valuable uses of technology, there are also risks to our children and to their psychological well-being. Being aware of those consequences will help as we move forward in a more balanced approach in our relationships with and without technology.

3. Adopt a family philosophy of 'cyber balance'

It is critical that families adopt a lifestyle that is not entirely built around technology. As is true of the foods we put into our bodies, what we feed our minds will affect our levels of emotional wellbeing and connectedness. Parents/guardians must adopt a family philosophy of balancing their use of technology with other family routines (Trolley & Hanel, 2010).

- Begin with a family assessment. By asking some tough questions, take an honest inventory of your family's use of technology.
    - ➢ Is there healthy balance of use of technology in your home?
    - ➢ How much time are family members spending on various devices?
    - ➢ How much time are you spending together as a family or as individuals without the use of technology?
    - ➢ Do the quantity and quality of technological use interfere with being present and available for one another?

- Set up family guidelines to implement *cyber balance*.

> ➤ Designate periods of time during the day where no technology is allowed. Suggestions include meal time, car or travel time, and/or in the evenings when homework and chores are done.

> ➤ Designate "zones" and "times" that are "tech free." Honor those commitments!

> ➤ Take time during the weekend to have a "tech-free" day. Have a family day of doing chores, planning fun activities that do not include technology, and/or just spending time together.

> ➤ As a family, frequently revisit topics of accepting responsibility and accountability for one's actions in the cyber world and the real world.

> ➤ As a family, brainstorm other ways to implement *cyber balance*.

4. Find ways in your family to experience direct interaction, to empathize with one another, and to serve others

To combat the online norms of indirect interaction, of detachment from one another, and of self-serving behaviors, we must plan and implement healthy social behaviors (Trolley & Hanel, 2010). The following activities will help to promote direct interaction, to nurture empathy for one another, and to create opportunities to serve others.

- During the designated "tech-free" periods, take time to be present and available for one another. Talk together face to face, without interrupting. Really listen to each other. Give each member of the family time to share ideas, thoughts and feelings.

- Replace "tech games" with real-life activities, sports, hobbies, or games. Enjoy the person/s who are with you "in the present." Let them know how important they are.

- Each day or each week (at the minimum), do something good for someone in your family without being asked. Then, do something special for a friend, a peer, or someone you know who needs a helping hand. Look for ways to do good — an example to others.

- With your church, synagogue, mosque, temple, youth group, sports club, or favorite organization, seek out ways to help others who are less fortunate.

- Speak up or stand up for others who are being criticized, bullied, made fun of, or humiliated in any way. Don't stand and watch in silence; be a friend when a friend is needed.
- Seek out ways to be present and available for others.

5. Parents/Guardians, model the behaviors that you expect from your children

We have tremendous influence in our children's lives, at least early on, or until we prove ourselves to be unworthy of it. Model the balanced behaviors that you expect from your children. In return, they are more likely to respect you, and thus, are more willing to follow your lead.

Conclusion

Technology is here to stay, as it should be. Children will continue to embrace its magnificence while navigating through safe as well as dangerous territories. It is our duty to teach them how to protect them-selves from injury, and it is our responsibility to intervene when they need our support and help. Most importantly, in order to prevent them from experiencing the destructive antisocial side-effects from an over-indulgence of technology, we must guide, monitor, and balance their intake. This high-tech generation needs our best parenting; they deserve no less.

Part Two: Let's Tackle Screen Dependence

The Effects: How Did We Get Here?

This section may be difficult to read for those who raise children. Why? Because we, as caring adults, do not want to think we might be doing something that is contributing to the harm of our children. I want you to know, you are not responsible for what you don't know. And, most parents/guardians have no idea about the dangers of passive and interactive screen time on their children. Don't beat yourself up. Don't become immobilized in your guilt. Don't bury yourself in denial because your friends aren't changing their ways. Let's "Power Down." Let's turn off our electronics and turn our attention to the effects screen time is having on our children. Remember, real power comes from being informed.

"Power Down" — Focusing Attention on the Effects of Screen Time

Clinical Concerns and Behavioral Effects

According to Dr. Victoria Dunckley, author of *Reset Your Child's Brain*, "The truth is, research suggests that *all* screen activities provide unnatural stimulation to the nervous system and can cause adverse effects" (2015, p. 19). Dr. Dunckley, along with other experts, believes exposure to screens stimulates the brain's pleasure center, increasing levels of dopamine. The continual release of large amounts of dopamine has a number of clinical concerns and behavioral effects.

1. Clinical Concerns — Electronic Screen Syndrome and Other Related Disorders

Dr. Dunckley is the first to identify a new disorder — Electronic Screen Syndrome. "Children may show symptoms of Electronic Screen Syndrome — a state of dysregulation where children lack the ability to modulate mood, attention, and/or levels of arousal in a manner appropriate to the given environment or stimulus" (Dunckley, 2015, p. 16). Dr. Dunckley states, "...the greater the stimulation — in the form of changing scenes, vivid colors, rapid or sudden movements, multitasking, or multimodal sensory input — and the more often that stimulation occurs, the harder it is to regulate arousal..." (2015, p. 19). Dr. Dunckley and other experts also believe that as children remain in a state of over-stimulation and hyper-arousal, they experience tremendous stress, which also contributes to symptoms of irritability, depression, mood swings, tantrums, and outright aggression. According to Dr. Nicholas Kardaras, "They may also demonstrate poor impulse control and low frustration tolerance" (2016, pp. 89-90).

Over the years, there has been a dramatic increase in diagnosed cases of Attention Deficit Disorder (ADD) and Attention Deficit Hyperactivity Disorder (ADHD). Experts agree that many children may be misdiagnosed and medicated unnecessarily, and/or these disorders may be exacerbated by exposure to screens. "'Acquired Attention-Deficit Disorder' is a term coined by Dr. John Ratey, Clinical Professor of Psychiatry at Harvard Medical School, which describes how too much screen time was rewiring kids' brains" (Kersting, 2016, pp. 4-5). Thus, children's symptoms, which closely mimic ADD or ADHD, may instead be the consequences of screen exposure.

2. Clinical Concerns — Recreational Use, Abuse, or Addiction

Although many parents have heard the terms "Internet Addiction," "Gaming Addiction," or "Screen Addiction," they may wonder if these terms are legitimate. According to addiction specialist, Dr. Nicholas Kardaras, "...brain development is a fragile process that can easily be disrupted by both brain under-stimulation and over-stimulation" (2016, p. 18). Experts are in agreement that both tech and gaming addiction are directly correlated to the release of large amounts of dopamine, the primary brain chemical associated with reward pathways activated by addiction (Dunckley, 2015).

When behaviors move from the realm of recreational usage to problematic usage (where there is resistance to stopping the behavior or abstaining from it), or abuse (when other areas of life are being neg-atively affected) or dependence (where there are issues of tolerance and withdrawal in conjunction with resistance and adverse effects), this is cause for serious concern. It is very difficult to admit if your child may have moved from the realm of recreational use to problematic abuse or dependence. If we, as adults, are having a hard time putting down our technology or curbing our screen time, imagine how challenging it is for youngsters, whose brains are still forming and becoming conditioned to the flow of dopamine highs.

3. Behavioral Effects

Behavioral effects include irritability, inability to calm down, tantrums, distractibility, and aggression, especially after lengthy periods of time spent interacting with screens. On a more serious behavioral spectrum, many children show symptoms of depression, anxiety, impulsivity, as well as other mood and conduct disorders. Dr. Dunckley also points out that along with the dysregulation of dopamine levels, other neurotransmitters are disrupted, such as serotonin, which is paramount in maintaining socialization, stable mood, a sense of well-being, and coping with stress. Dr. Dunckley further explains, "Late-at-night light may further depress mood, both because serotonin is made from melatonin (which is suppressed by light), and because sleep disturbance itself is linked to mood issues" (2015, p. 59). Consequently, countless young people are presenting with sleep disturbance issues and sleep disorders, not only affecting their moods and behaviors but also impacting their cognitive abilities.

This is important. Our children are being raised on a large diet of technology. Many of them spend up to nine or more hours a day on their screens, not including school time (Common Sense Media, 2016). With both passive (observing) and interactive (engaging with) screen time, along with the glow from screens, we now know there are significant neurological and clinical effects. In Dr. Kardaras' words, these effects are "Even more so for children with still-developing brains not equipped to handle that level of stimulation" (2016, p. 3).

Psychological and Emotional Effects

It is only natural to pay attention to children's physical or behavioral changes. We witness them, whether appropriate or not, and we intervene accordingly. It is trickier to notice the psychological and emotional effects, because these changes may evolve over time with subtle alterations in mood, affect, or behavior. Also, because our children are constantly growing and developing, some of their moodiness or sensitivities are just a natural part of the process. However, as they continue to spend increasing amounts of time on their screens, becoming more and more dependent upon them for their social communications and interactions, unfortunately, they may also experience negative psychological and emotional effects. As parents, we must pay close attention to the following.

1. Impact on Self-Esteem and Self-Worth

This is a huge issue. Because our children have access 24/7 to their networks and social sites, they are constantly assessing themselves in relationship to others and to external influences. They evaluate themselves and their worth by the number of likes, followers, friends, retweets, views, etc. Experts have termed this *social comparison*. And although we, too, experienced this growing up, we did not have to deal with the chronic stress of knowing whether we measured up or we good enough because of an unrelenting supply of artificial sources of validation. It has been well documented that the more time children (and adults) spend on social sites such as Facebook, their levels of depression increase, while their self-worth is lower (Kardaras, 2016). To compound the stress experienced from social comparison, Dr. Kathy Koch describes, "Many [young people] have FOMO — the fear of missing out. They want to know what's going on as its happening. NOW" (2015, p. 107). This unnatural need to be constantly connected not only exacerbates anxiety, but also creates a false sense of belonging and further tethers children's worth to fleeting superficial messaging.

2. Impact on Emotional Intelligence (EQ)

"Emotional intelligence is the ability to use, understand, and manage emotions in a productive, healthy way. It is what helps us communicate effectively, empathize with others, and overcome life's challenges" (Kersting, 2016, p. 63). In order to develop strong EQ, the front part of the brain — the prefrontal cortex — must have a healthy development. Research is validating how chronic screen exposure negatively affects this development by weakening the neural circuits that send messages to the prefrontal cortex. The prefrontal cortex controls executive functioning, facilitating skills such as decision-making and regulating impulse control. Children with lower EQs experience anxiety, depression, and lack resilience. Consequently, there is an overall sense of helplessness or fear of failure (Kersting, 2016).

3. Impact on Social Skills

This effect may sound strange when kids spend many hours a day in constant contact with their friends, but the social skills of how to interact indirectly will not serve them well in the real world. Without the practice of face to face interaction, which requires eye contact and the ability to read social cues, children experience social anxiety in real life interactions. As we discussed in Part One: Let's Tackle Cyber Bullying, excessive time spent in indirect communication or interaction cultivates a sense of disconnect with another human being, resulting in an inability to feel empathy for others and to make healthy, intimate connections.

4. Impact on Life Messages

Just as we did, as today's children grow and develop, they learn about themselves and their environments from their life experiences, which translate into life messages — the internal dialogue we say to ourselves about who we are and how we feel about our world. For example, if a child grows up in a nurturing, affirming, and validating environment, the internalized life messages may be *I am a good person. I live in a safe place. I am capable.* In an abusive, neglectful, or unstable environment, life messages may be internalized as *I cannot trust anyone. I don't matter.* These life messages are powerful because they fuel our attitudes and actions. This is very important. Children who raised by technology, in lieu of with it (Koch, 2015), receive maladaptive life messages, which in turn rob them of developing life skills needed in the real world.

In Dr. Kathy Koch's book, *Screens and Teens: Connecting With Our Kids In A Wireless World,* she maps out five harmful life messages. Although I believe all of them are important, three of the most detrimental are the following:

1. I am the center of my own universe;

2. I deserve to be happy all the time;

3. I must have choices (2015).

Those entrusted with the welfare of children are witnessing the manifestations of those harmful life messages. Learning who they are and about their environments primarily from their interactive and passive screen time cultivates an extremely narcissistic, self-centered, entitled, impatient, and anxious population of children (Kersting, 2016; Koch, 2015).

5. Impact on Psycho-Social Development

What I am about to say may sound harsh. So, please take a deep breath... One of the advantages of technology and screen-to-screen contact is that we can connect with our children 24/7. One of the disadvantages is we can connect with them 24/7!

When children are constantly connected to parents who are micro-managing their lives and shadowing their every movement, their psycho-social development will be arrested or at the very least slowed. We see growing evidence of this in the following examples:

- Students who cannot complete their own homework

- Teens who cannot make a decision without fear of failing

- College students who are dropping out at alarming rates, lacking the life skills to perform on their own
- Young adults who do not know how to apply for a job, conduct themselves in an interview, or compete in the workforce.

The natural process of individuating and differentiating from one's family is paramount to healthy psychological and social development. Children must be given space from parental monitoring and management in order to develop a strong sense of identity and self-efficacy. Their psychological and emotional development needs to be a priority of parenting. We must pay attention to how young people view themselves and their world, both online and offline. This is going to mean that we, as adults, also shift our tech habits and behaviors. We do need to be present and available in order to pay attention to them and their needs, but not so "screen-attached" that we rob them of the opportunity to grow and flourish. We will discuss this further in the "Parent Up" section.

Brain Damage and Cognitive Effects

Although scientists are in agreement that more research is needed in the area of brain damage and cognitive effects due to screen exposure, studies over the past several years provide us with a window into the seriousness in this area. For the purposes of "Power Down & Parent Up," we will touch upon them briefly. Expand your knowledge by reading any of the experts referenced in the bibliography.

1. Response to Reward

Have you ever wondered why it is so hard to walk away from a slot machine? Have you ever felt a surge of adrenaline when you are exercising and thought you could go on forever? Have you experienced a rush when your post, tweet, text or upload received tons of likes, shares, or retweets? Have you or your children had a difficult time turning off a video game, wanting to achieve that elusive goal or score? If you answered yes to any of the above, please know, you are not alone!

Our brains are hard-wired to respond to reward. And we know that one of the most powerful ways of keeping us hooked to a game, or checking our social sites, or constantly texting, or whatever the habitual behavior may be is to provide intermittent, random, or scheduled positive reinforcement. Whether we are engaging in a behavior or consuming a substance, when our brain's reward pathways are activated, we want to continue. Although it may seem harmless at first to spend hours playing games or interacting on our screens, as our brains become conditioned to receiving those dopamine surges, we will want to return to them because it makes us feel good. Thus, whether it is in a video game, on a social site, or almost any on-line behavior, product developers are purposely designing them to keep us coming back. In a recent article, "Tristan Harris Believes Silicon Valley Is Addicting us to our Phones. He's Determined to Make It Stop" (*Atlantic Monthly*, Nov. 2016, p. 58), Harris, a former product philosopher at Google, states, "In short, we have lost our control of our relationship with technology because technology has become better at controlling us."

Limiting the degree of time kids spend using their technology has nothing to do with putting a damper on their fun or curbing their social life. It has everything to do with protecting their brains from early addictive conditioning.

2. Role of White Matter in the Brain and Its Relationship to Neural Pruning

Please don't allow the words "white matter" and "neural pruning" to discourage you. I will keep this simple. I'm not a scientist either! This section is really important.

We have gray matter in our brains, but we also have white matter, myelin, which functions as our neural network. According to Dr. Kardaras, myelin is important because, "Myelination occurs as part of a healthy developmental process. As we grow and learn, our myelination increases in areas of the brain that need it" (2015, p. 64). Just as with our bodies, how we train our brains and what they are exposed to or conditioned by will determine their pathways of future direction and/or disturbance.

For example, a child who learns reading will typically be a strong reader. A child who has been instructed in performing arts, visual arts, or sports early in life will most likely exhibit talents in those areas as he/she grows and strengthens those pathways. On the contrary, if there are deficits in a child's upbringing or damaging influences, these will inhibit healthy pathways of myelination. Inherent within the process of myelination is the concept of "use-it-or-lose it" (Kardaras, 2015). In other words, just as with our bodies, the areas of the brain we train the hardest will be most affected and altered, positively or negatively, whereas the areas least utilized will wither and weaken. In his book, *Disconnected*, Thomas Kersting explains, "Neural pruning is a natural and normal occurrence during adolescence, and it is the brain's way of weeding out pathways that are used less often" (2016, p. 8).

Thus, not only does over-exposure to screens alter the formation of pathways but "...the over-stimulation of the glowing, flashing screens of iPads and video games can damage myelin in neural pathways..." (Kardaras, 2015, p. 65). In *Glow Kids*, Dr. Kardaras describes some of the problems associated with over-stimulation during key developmental periods for children:

1. the inability to pay attention and focus;
2. the inability to feel empathy; and
3. the inability to discern reality (2015).

Other experts such as Thomas Kersting also contend that neural pruning produces additional consequences:

1. a struggle to communicate face to face;
2. poor coping skills with real life; and
3. a short-circuiting effect in children's brains... creating a host of mental and emotional disorders (2016).

Parents/guardians, we are diligent about what our children put into their bodies and how they treat them. We need to be equally concerned about how our children's brains are neurologically wired and what we allow them to consume.

3. Ramifications of Multi-Tasking and Task-Switching

Over the years, as our dependence and reliance upon electronic devices have increased, adults and youth have prided themselves in being able to multi-task or task-switch. While working on a document or task, we talk on the phone or answer texts as they come in. We check our email while watching TV or playing a video game. We listen to music while doing our work or homework, while keeping our phones near in case someone is trying to reach us. We sit in a classroom or workshop, secretly checking our messages or playing a game. In study after study, experts have discovered that although multi-taskers feel they are doing well on all of their tasks, in fact they are not.

In a *Time Magazine* special edition article "Devices Mess With Your Brain" (December 2016, p .37), author Markham Heid reported, "One study found it can take your brain 15 to 25 minutes to get back to where it was after stopping to check an email. In fact, people who judged themselves to be expert digital multi-taskers tended to be pretty bad at it." Additionally, Heid found the results of one study suggested, "people who spend a lot of time 'media multi-tasking' — or juggling lots of different websites, apps, programs, or other digital stimuli — tend to have less gray matter in a part of their brain involved with thought and emotion control" (2016, p. 37). While mature adult brains are being affected to varying degrees, our concern is for children whose young, developing brains are not equipped to handle the chronic stimulation accompanied by continual interruption of focus and attention.

If you have wondered why your children have a hard time sticking with one activity at a time or maintaining focus on one task at a time, it isn't their fault. Their brains are being conditioned to jump around or task-switch. Experts are in agreement that constant task-switching negatively affects executive functioning. In *Disconnected,* Thomas Kersting (2016), has coined the phrase "fragmented thinking," and describes the following characteristics among children:

- Short attention
- Fractured focus
- Poor memory, social skills, and interpersonal skills
- Problems with learning and completing school work

Contrary to popular belief, multi-tasking and task-switching are nothing to brag about. As with many unhealthy behaviors, it is only natural to justify it is because everyone is doing it.

~ ~ ~

As we bring this section to a close, understanding why and how our children's brains and well-being are affected is not easy to digest. You might be feeling unsettled by this information. You might want to dismiss and disregard it, because like most responsible parents/guardians, you would never want to do anything which would be detrimental to your children's behavioral, psychological, social, and neurological development. Take a deep breath. Give yourself a break. And then, get ready to "Parent Up"! Get ready to make healing and healthy changes.

Part Three: Raising Tech-Healthy Children

It's Never Too Late

Recently, I gave a workshop-"How To Be A Good Digital Parent" (FOSI, 2016) to a local elementary school PTA gathering. As I was talking about the importance of limiting time spent on screens, a mother sitting close to me raised her hand. I waited as she spoke. Her voice was quivering. "I have been allowing my eight year old son to spend hours every day playing games. It keeps him quiet while I'm trying to get things done. You see, he has ADD and I'm a single mom. It's really hard." I listened. She hesitated and bravely asked, "Is it too late?"

My heart sank as her eyes watered. I gently responded, "It is never... I repeat... never... too late."

Change is never easy. I often say, "Anything worthwhile rarely is." And, creating healthy change in our children's screen behaviors is going to require us do the same. Let's get started as we "Parent Up" — Taking Control of our Children's Health: Embracing Seven Proactive Practices and Four Healthy Guidelines.

"Parent Up" — Taking Control of our Children's Health: Embracing Seven Proactive Practices

Step One: Parent up by powering down

We need to do the same work we are going to ask of our children. Any time they see our hypocrisy, they will resist and resent change. In a 2016 study by Common Sense Media, "28% of teens feel their parents are addicted to their mobile devices and 41% of teens feel their parents get distracted by devices and don't pay attention when they are together" (Felt & Robb, pp. 2-3).

> ➢ Right now, make a commitment to yourself and your family that you are going to participate in making healthy changes with your screen behaviors. Say it. Write it down and place it where everyone will see it.

Step Two: Parent up by preparing family

Once your commitment is in place, parent up by preparing family members. This is an opportunity to bring the family together to explain your concerns about screen exposure and talk about what you have learned. Children are typically more interested in the "why" than the "what." So, take your time and talk to them age appropriately. At all costs, avoid statements like, "We are doing this because I said so." Let them know the entire family will be working on this together. Let them know you are going to move slowly, a little at time, and you will invite their input and feedback.

> ➤ Set a time for a meeting to prepare your family. Then, introduce and implement Step Three.

Step Three: Parent up with a family assessment

Although we discussed "Adopt a family philosophy of cyber balance" in the previous section on cyber bullying (pp. 1-12) and we briefly outlined some guidelines, conducting an informal assessment is fun. More importantly, it helps the family to set their goals.

Get a piece of paper and make a chart for each family member. Use the template below, or design one. For each person, log in the time spent on various screens in the different time periods for each day of the week. For now, do not include time in classrooms for children or work commitments for adults. However, if screen time is being used for pleasure during school or work, log it in as well. Do this for one week. Be honest! And by the way, do not do this on a computer or laptop or phone!

Mom's Screen Usage

	Mon	Tue	Wed	Thur	Fri	Sat	Sun
6 - 9 am							
9 am - 12 pm							
12 - 4 pm							
4 - 7 pm							
7 - 10 pm							
10 pm - 6 am							

> ➤ Take a family assessment for one week!

Step Four: Parent up with goal setting to reduce screen time

After one week of assessment, calculate everyone's total hours of usage. With screen logs in hand, come together as a family to set goals for reducing screen time. Remember, whenever we are changing behaviors, it is wise to set reasonable goals. For example, cut back screen time by two hours a day to start. Do this for one week. Then, cut one or two more hours for the following week. And so on.

Many parents/guardians are shocked to learn the American Academy of Pediatrics recommends no more than two hours per day on screens for children. Newborns should not be exposed to screens and for infants 18-24 months, it is recommended screen time be accompanied by adult interaction. Therefore, I am going to suggest several healthy guidelines as families implement their goals for cutting back. Experts are in agreement on the following:

1. All screens must be kept in one room at home, preferably a living area or common family room. This keeps the family together, helps with monitoring and supervision of usage, and promotes more face to face communication and social inter-action.

2. No screens during meal times.

3. No screens allowed in bedrooms, ever. This includes adults.

4. No screen exposure two hours before bedtime.

> ➢ Set goals for one week reducing screen time. At the weekly family meeting, discuss what is working well and what is not. Talk about how to support and help one another. Reward your successes by spending time together, face to face, doing purposeful or pleasurable activities. Keep going, adjusting your goals for the next week. Repeat the process. Introduce Step Five, if it is not already in place.

Step Five: Parent Up with a Family Online Safety Contract

If your family does not already have a Family Online Safety Contract or a screen-use agreement in place, now is the time to establish one. Please refer to page 3 for specific guidelines. Because we know how important it is to limit our screen exposure, be sure to include goals for reducing screen time, as well as accountability measures. As children grow and mature, amend and adjust as they show responsibility. However, never lose sight of the detrimental effects on their developing minds.

> ➢ Implement a Family Online Safety Contract.

Step Six: Parent Up with replacing screen time with family, outdoor fun, and face to face time

As we continue to "Power Down & Parent Up," it is important to replace screen time with other activities. It is easy to fall back into previous patterns unless we have planned and prepared for their replacement. Please refer to pp. 10-12 for suggestions. Also, sit down with your children. Talk with them and find out what is important for them. Involve them in the planning.

> ➢   Replace screen time with other activities

Step Seven: Parent Up with a positive approach to resistance

You might be thinking right now, "My kids are going to flip out! They will be so mad!" And, you are probably right! When they roll their eyes, or slam their doors, or throw tantrums, remain positive and strong in your stance. Remember what you are learning. Love them when they are not being lovable. Love them by explaining why. Remember, despite what your children say or do, YOU remain the most important and influential person in their lives. Do not let them down by caving in! Continue to "Parent Up"!

> ➢   Use a positive approach to resistance.

"Parent Up" — Taking Control of our Children's Health: Embracing Four Healthy Guidelines

Healthy Guideline One: Parent up with going against the flow

I am frequently asked, "Holli, how old should my child be before I give him/her a smart phone?" Or, "When do you think a child should be allowed to be on social net-working sites?" I usually answer, "The degree of access or exposure to or consumption of *anything* is a predictor to the degree of consequence — either positive or negative." Thus, it is my belief the earlier we expose children to screens or allow them access to social sites, games, etc., the more likely they are to experience harmful consequences. Going against the flow is not easy. You are raising your children, not technology. My recommendations include the following:

1.   Although most social networking sites require users to be thirteen, delay this until age fifteen.

2.   Many children under age twelve are using smart phones. I recommend age sixteen. Children, tweens, and adolescents can

use a 'dumb phone' for texting/calling and a laptop/computer for schoolwork, etc.

3. At all ages, monitor and supervise usage, even texts. Refer to pp. 3-4. This can be done respectfully through the use of the Family Online Safety Contract. A kid's typical pressure will be: "Everyone in class has a smartphone. They'll laugh at me for having this old piece of junk! I won't have any friends!" etc. You need to deal with this tactic.

Please remember, not only are young people's developing brains susceptible to dependence and injury from screen exposure, but their pre-frontal cortex, which controls executive functioning, does not fully form until mid to late twenties. It is unfair and unsafe to expect them to navigate the cyber world with all its inherent dangers and temptations when they do not possess the capacity to do so.

> ➢ Go against the flow and train your kids to resist peer pressure.

Healthy Guideline Two: Parent up with conversations about real worth and cyber worth

Under the section on "psychological and emotional effects," we learned how children are being heavily conditioned by their online environments and interactions. As a Marriage and Family Therapist, of all the health consequences associated with screen time, this one concerns me the most. Why? First, I believe as children attach their worth or esteem predominantly to external, artificial, and fleeting sources of influence, they will undermine the process of learning how to cultivate their internal, authentic, and sustainable sources of value. In short, when their worth is constantly determined by others, there is no need to define their own. Second, children (as do adults) make decisions based on their assessment of their self-worth. Children who think well of themselves typically feel less pressure to fit in, and they tend to make healthy choices. Children who feel poorly about themselves believe they have less to lose, want to be accepted by others, and often are drawn to risky behaviors.

I am so passionate about this topic I wrote a novel, *Another Way*, for tweens–teens and for you! I encourage you to pick up a copy and have an ongoing conversation with your children about the power of self-worth. For now, I offer a few suggestions for starting a conversation:

1. Worth is based on what is important to us. Ask your children what is important to them and why, both in their real world and cyber world.

2. Talk about their real worth and their cyber worth. Is it the same? Is it different? Why?

3. Talk about how real friends differ from cyber friends, followers, fake friends. Or if they do differ?

4. Given the various ages of children and the importance of belonging or fitting in, explore with them how they feel about themselves. Do they feel important? Do they feel they matter? Do they feel valuable? Ask them what they need from you. Most importantly, help them to discover their own worth.

> ➤ Talk about their worth — real and cyber.

Healthy Guideline Three: Parent up with two powerful gifts

Parents and guardians possess two powerful "Parent Up" gifts. They require one thing of us: we continue to power down.

Gift One: Whenever you can and as often as possible, give your full attention to your children. By giving our attention, we message to them that they are important.

A few examples include:

1. When they speak, look them in their eyes. Listen. Ask questions.

2. When they want to show or share something, stop what you are doing and watch. Validate and affirm. Encourage them.

3. Spend time before bed each night with each child, reading, sharing, praying, holding one another, and giving them your complete undivided attention.

Gift Two: While giving children quality attention signals that they are valuable and important, we do not want to confuse this gift with giving them more than is healthy. As was discussed in psycho-social effects, we want to facilitate their healthy individuation: trust, autonomy, initiative, industry, and identity. In doing so, we need to screen-detach from them and give them opportunities to discover who they are on their own. As our children grow and develop, it is critical they are allowed:

1. To succeed, and to learn from their failures

2. To have your support when needed, and to go it alone when called to do so

3. To win and to lose

4. To discover with ease and to persist even when it's frustrating

5. To have you guide their decisions and allow them to make their own

6. To have your protection and to earn their independence and autonomy

> ➢ Give the gifts of attention and of individuation

Healthy Guideline Four: Parent up with support from physicians, school counselors, therapists, and screen dependence experts

In covering the multitude of screen effects on youngsters, you may be wondering if your child is suffering from any number of behavioral, psychological, or neurological disturbances or disorders. You may question if the child's symptoms or diagnoses were precipitated or exacerbated by exposure to screens. Or you may have serious concerns about screen abuse, dependence, and addiction, especially in the area of video gaming.

In order to get an accurate assessment as to what is going on with your child, it is important to determine how much or to what degree exposure to screens is playing a role in your child's current wellbeing and/or in conjunction with co-occurring disorders. Please follow the suggestions below.

1. Implement each step of the Proactive Practices. Allow at least one month or until screen time has been drastically reduced. Then, reassess concerns.

2. Implement the healthy guidelines and monitor any changes, positive or negative. Reassess after one month.

3. Contact your physician and schedule a complete physical to rule out any physiological or organic conditions.

4. If behavioral, psychological, and/or emotional problems persist and/or there is clearly an addiction issue, contact a school counselor or licensed therapist/psychologist for a thorough assessment, treatment plan, and referrals.

Finally, continue to support yourself by turning to our experts on screen dependence. I highly recommend several of the books referenced in "Power Down & Parent Up:"

1. *Disconnected: How To Reconnect With Our Digitally Distracted Kids* by Thomas Kersting

2. *Teens and Screens: Connecting with our Children in a Wireless World* by Dr. Kathy Koch

3. *Reset Your Child's Brain: A Four-Week Plan To End Meltdowns, Raise Grades, And Boost Social Skills by Reversing The Effects of Electronic Screen-Time* by Dr. Victoria Dunckley

4. *Glow Kids: How Screen Addiction is Hijacking Our Kids – And How To Break The Trance* by Dr. Nicholas Kardaras

5. *Another Way: A Novel* by Holli Kenley

> ➢   Rule out and seek support.

Let's Show Them They Matter More Than Our Screens

Recently, while I was waiting for a delayed flight in the San Francisco Airport, I watched as a little boy politely and patiently tried to get his dad's attention. Fixated to his screen, the dad was oblivious to his son. After a short time, the little guy, who was playing with his trucks on the floor, turned to me and held up his yellow truck. I smiled and asked him if it was his favorite. The dad, slightly startled, looked up at me.

I gently spoke. "Your little boy is so patient and he entertains himself so well. May I ask how old he is?"

The dad replied. "He just turned five."

"Oh", I said, glancing at the happy little guy. "My daughter will be thirty-seven next month." And with a lump forming in my throat, I added, "The time goes by so fast."

The dad put down his phone, got on the floor, and began interacting with his son. His little boy squealed with delight.

Parents and guardians, together we can protect, intervene, and prevent cyber bullying; and we can address and correct unhealthy attitudes, behaviors, and feelings that promote screen dependence. We can raise tech-healthy children. Let's show them they matter more than our screens. Let's...

"Power Down & Parent Up!"

Face to Face: Unwired

It was last summer, but I remember as if it were yesterday,
The image forever etched upon my soul.
A family gathered together sharing barbeque with close friends,
No technology to fill the space — only conversation and eager ears.

With plates of lean steak, bowls of salads, and baskets of breads passed among us,
The young adults home from college filled their bellies and we ours.
Dad bantered with his grown children and laughter sprinkled over the table,
No technology to distract attention — focus on the speaker and minds present.

The flow of food and drink continued for hours and yet it flew by,
Family stories told from years past and we too told our own.
Mom's nurturing spirit brought warmth to more delicate conversation,
No technology to interrupt the flow of empathy — each person available for the other.

Stomachs beckoned for a pause, but soon desserts galore arrived,
And a calm settled in as the sun started to disappear.
Plans, dreams, and hopes were explored — each creating a sparkle,
No technology to dim the glow — similar visions captured and shared by all.

Darkness came too quickly as final words embraced the night,
With winks and spars, young adults took their cues to clear and to clean.
Older adults were left to say their thanks, goodbyes, and next-times,
No technology still — only eyes on eyes and arms reaching for hugs.

Walking to our car, I felt full for the first time in a long while,
Realizing that what I devoured was so rare, so missed, so needed.
No social pathogens — just hungry hearts feasting on a buffet of human connection,
And savoring each and every morsel of being — of simply being present for one another.

About the Author

Holli Kenley is a California State Licensed Marriage and Family Therapist and a California Licensed Teacher. She holds a Masters Degree in Psychology with an emphasis in Marriage, Family, and Child Counseling. She first became interested in promoting the wellness of others in the early 1990s by volunteering time to lead support groups for women struggling with Premenstrual Dysphoric Disorder (PMDD). This experience was the motivation behind her first book, *The PMS Puzzle*, as well as the impetus to return to graduate school to become a licensed therapist.

Holli has worked in a variety of settings: a women's shelter and transitional housing, a counseling center, and in private practice. Counseling with adolescents, teens, young and older adults, Holli's areas of special training and interest include sexual trauma and abuse, betrayal, addiction, codependency, and cyber bullying. Holli is the author of numerous published articles and several books including *Breaking Through Betrayal: And Recovering the Peace Within, 2nd Edition* (2016), *Another Way: A Novel* (2015), *Mountain Air: Relapsing and Finding The Way Back…One Breath at a Time* (2013), and *Cyber Bullying No More* (2011).

In the field of psychology, Holli is a nationally recognized author, speaker and workshop presenter. She has been five–time peer presenter at the California Association of Marriage and Family Therapists' Annual State Conferences, speaking on Cyber Bullying, Betrayal, Relapse, and Sexual Abuse Recovery. Holli has appeared on over one hundred podcasts and is a frequent TV guest speaking on issues of wellness.

Prior to and during her work as a therapist, Holli taught in public education for thirty years. Holli and her husband reside in the mountains of Arizona.

To find out more about Holli's work or to contact her
for workshops, conferences, or speaking opportunities, please visit
www.HolliKenley.com

Follow on Twitter @HolliKenley

Stop by her Facebook page www.facebook.com/AuthorHolliKenley

Bibliography

Alter, A. (2017). *Irresistible: The rise of addictive technology and the business of keeping us hooked.* New York, NY: Penguin Press.

Ang, R. P., & Goh, D. H. (August 2010). Cyberbullying among adolescents: The role of affective and cognitive empathy, and gender. *Child Psychiatry and Human Development,* 41, 4, 387-397.

Bosker, B. (2016). Tristan Harris believes silicon valley is addicting us to our phones: He's determined to make it stop. *The Atlantic ,* (November), 56-65.

Coloroso, B. (2004). *The bully, the bullied and the bystander.* New York: HarperCollins.

Doan , A. P., M.D., Ph.D., & Strickland, B. (2012). *Hooked on games: The lure and cost of video game and internet addiction.* Coraville , IA : F.E.P. International, Inc.

Dunckley, V. L., MD. (2015). *Reset your child's brain: A four-week plan to end meltdowns, raise grades, and boost social skills by reversing the effects of electronic screen-time.* Navato, CA: New World Library .

Dooley, J., Pyzalski, J. & Cross, D. (2009). Cyberbullying Versus Face-to-Face Bullying: A theoretical and conceptual review. *Zeitschrift fur psychologie/journal of psychology,* 217 (4), 182-188.

Felt , L. J., Ph.D., & Robb, M. B., Ph.D. (2016). Technology addiction: Concern, controversy, and finding balance. *Common Sense — Executive Summary,* (May), 3-13. Retrieved January, 2017.

Grossman , D., Lt. Col., & DeGaetano, G. (2014). *Stop teaching our kids to kill: A call to action against TV, movie and video game violence.* (Second ed.). New York, NY: Harmony Books (Crown).

Heid, M. (2016). Devices mess with your brain... Is your smartphone affecting your mind? Yes — and you're probably suffering from phantom text syndrome, too. *Time - Special Edition,* 34-37.

Hinduja, S., & Patchin, J. W. (2009). *Bullying beyond the schoolyard: Preventing and responding to cyberbullying.* Thousand Oaks, Calif: Corwin Press.

Kabali , H. K., M.D., Irigoyen, M. M., M.D., Nunez-Davis, R., D.O., M.P.H., Budacki, J. G., D.O., Mohanty, S. H., M.D., Leister, K. P., M.D., & Bonner, R. L., Jr., M.D. (2015). Exposure and use of mobile media devices by young children. *American Academy of Pediatrics, 136*(6). Retrieved January 10, 2017.

Patchin, J., & Hinduja, S. (2011). *Cyberbullying prevention and response: expert perspectives.* New York, NY: Routledge.

Kardaras, N., PhD. (2016). *Glow kids: How screen addiction is hijacking our kids-and how to break the trance.* (First ed.). New York , NY: St. Martin's Press.

Kersting, T. (2016). *Disconnected: How to reconnect our digitally distracted kids.* USA: Thomas Kersting.

Koch, K., Ph.D. (2015). *Screens and teens: connecting with our kids in a wireless world.* Chicago, IL: Moody.

Li, Q. (January 2010). Cyberbullying in High Schools: A Study of Students' Behaviors and Beliefs about This New Phenomenon. *Journal of Aggression in Maltreatment and Trauma,* 19, (4), 372-292.

Strasburger , V. C., M.D., FAAP, & Hogan, M. J., M.D, FAAP. (2013). Children, adolescents, and the media [Abstract]. *American Academy of Pediatrics, 132*(November), 958-961. Retrieved January 10, 2017.

Trolley, B., & Hanel, C. (2010). *Cyber kids, cyber bullying, cyber balance.* Thousand Oaks, Calif: Corwin Press.

Index

High School. Dating. Sex...
14 year old Chloe Wheeler wonders - *is she ready?*

Finding it uncomfortable talking with her parents, Chloe turns to her best friend—Amanda Hill. Searching for guidance, they attend a nondenominational youth group where Pastor Rick Summers is facilitating a series of talks on sex entitled Another Way.

At the first group meeting, Chloe meets football star Tyrell Fields. As they begin dating and Chloe's feelings intensify, she grabs hold of the lessons of *Another Way* and discovers...

- Her worth.
- Her voice.
- Her levels of readiness.
- Her power to make healthy decisions.

"Holli Kenley beautifully shares in *Another Way* how young people can embrace confidence and self-empowerment as they find their way through the challenges of the teen years."
    Cathy Taughinbaugh– Parent Coach, Helping Parents Find Peace

"*Another Way* is an indispensable book for teens and those who care about them...Holli Kenley has done it again with this practical, entertaining, and bold book"
    Jill Osborne, Eds, LPC, RPT– Helping Families Reconnect

"*Another Way* introduces our young readers to a new way of thinking. Through self-discovery and self-empowerment, Chloe learns there truly is Another Way--a way to stand strong with honesty and personal integrity."
        Judy Herzanek– Changing Lives Foundation

"*Another Way* is one of those great reads that is sure to find an audience with readers of all ages."
        Cyrus Webb – Host of Conversations LIVE,
        Editor-in-Chief *Conversations Magazine*

Available at www.amazon.com/author/hollikenley

Are you ready to heal?

Breaking Through Betrayal: And Recovering the Peace Within is for any individual who has experienced betrayal and is struggling to break through its bonds. Through a proven process tailored for recovery from betrayal injury, readers are invited to:

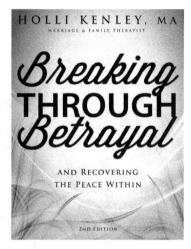

- Explore and connect with the different kinds of betrayal: rejection or abandonment; a violation of trust; a shattered truth or belief.
- Identify and move through confusion, worthlessness, and powerlessness while uncovering contributors of symptom intensity and duration.
- Revive and restore mind, body, and spirit with a 5-part recovering process for "righting oneself" and attend to re-occurrence or re-injury.

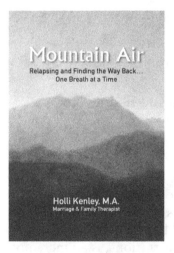

Deep down inside, each of us knows what our truths are. It is forgivable to lose them... it is unforgivable not to reclaim them... *Mountain Air: Relapsing And Finding The Way Back One Breath At A Time* is a brutally honest personal narrative detailing a painful decent into relapse and a powerful journey back to recovering. Without condemnation but with passion and purpose, Mountain Air...

- Embraces individuals who have abandoned their authentic ways of being for a life of personal neglect, indulgence, or self-destruction.
- Speaks to individuals who have betrayed their healing tenets - the addict who has lost his sobriety, the abused who has returned to her abuser, or the codependent who continues to rescue the uncontrollable.
- Reaches out to individuals who have maintained a life of stability and wellness, but who are eroding over time – and losing their sense of self and of spirit.

What's happening to me?

This book translates anxiety from the jargon of psychology into concrete experiences that children can relate to. Children and their parents will understand the biological and emotional components of anxiety responsible for the upsetting symptoms they experience. *Please Explain Anxiety to Me, 2nd Edition* gives accurate physiological information in child friendly language. A colorful dinosaur story explains the link between brain and body functioning, followed by practical therapeutic techniques that children can use to help themselves. Children will:

- learn that they can handle most issues if they are explained at their developmental level

- understand the brain/body connection underlying anxiety

- identify with the examples given

- find comfort and reassurance in knowing that others have the same experience

- be provided with strategies and ideas to help them change their anxiety responses

- be able to enjoy childhood and to give up unnecessary worrying

"On any given day, around thirty percent of my patients have anxiety related symptoms. The simplicity and completeness of the explanations and treatment of anxiety given in this book is remarkable. Defining the cause, treating the core symptoms, and most importantly bringing it to a child's level accompanied by wonderful illustrations, is an incredible feat. I will definitely use this book in my practice."

Zev Ash, M.D. F.A.A.P., Pediatrician

www.ingramcontent.com/pod-product-compliance
Lightning Source LLC
LaVergne TN
LVHW012201040326
832903LV00003B/47